SHINING
BUBBLES
OF THE SACRED ART

SHINING
BUBBLES
OF THE SACRED ART

DENIZÉ LAUTURE

CITI OF
BOOKS

CITIOFBOOKS, INC.
3736 Eubank NE Suite A1
Albuquerque, NM 87111-3579
www.citiofbooks.com
Hotline: 1 (877) 389-2759
Fax: 1 (505) 930-7244

Ordering Information:
Quantity sales. Special discounts are available on quantity purchases by corporations, associations, and others. For details, contact the publisher at the address above.

Printed in the United States of America.

ISBN-13:   Paperback   979-8-90124-142-4
             eBook   979-8-90124-143-1

Library of Congress Control Number: 2026902559

TABLE OF CONTENTS

Acknowledgments

This carefully chosen collection of poetry is gladly dedicated to my two grand-daughters Charleigh A. Lauture and Adiyah M. Lauture.

Also, I am sincerely grateful to Georgia Anderson and Zari Castro who worked tirelessly to produce the book.

Before the Word

Before the word there was the tune, the rhythm of the soul. The word came and borrowed the primal rhythm, and there was poetry, the verbal expression of the soul. The "poet" is its medium.

True Poetry is not simple

———————— ✛ ————————

True poetry is not simple. It has never been simple. It will never be simple. It will always be a heavy burden upon the shoulders of the poet-lamb, the only poet who creates true poetry. The burden multiplies if the poet is a native of a turmoil-ridden land. There are moments when the poet-lamb experiences fear, trembles, sheds tears at the slightest whisper of the muse.

I am a tiny vine
I need a tree
A good tree
To help me rise.

If at night I dream of poetry, in the morning I don't mind gnawing stale bread.

My pen, I always dip it in the lunar blood of the muse!

I was deep, truly deep into poetry. But a naked woman parted her thighs in front of me. I began combing pubic hair, instead of riming verses.

My unpublished manuscripts, like spirits of dead relatives or dead friends, one by one glide at night to torment me in my sleep.

A buzzing bee hangs in the air
Not far from the poet's ears
We will soon hear
Some stinging verses.

Poe-Tree!

Leaves that caress the poet's face
Fruits that fall into the poet's hands
Limbs that hug the melancholic poet
Barks that blend with the poet's skin
Roots that coil around the poet's ankles
Thorns that prick the poet's heart
Sap that anoints the poet's body and mind
And shade that always welcomes the beaten-up bard
Poetry!

Sucking Ballpoint Pens

❖

Good writers have their greatest moments of joy when sucking empty ballpoint pens they have used to the last ink drop.

Chosen Blacksmiths

Good poets are chosen blacksmiths
Well-trained in the divine art
Of hunting, catching, holding,
And molding fleeting rays
From the blazing furnaces
Of their consuming souls…

A Real Poet

A real poet is an enlightened bird, bizarre in its feathers, who knows how and where to place its beak to catch dewdrops that fall from the Muse's lips.

Masterful poets make the human heart throb and the human mind wonder with their use of language

Instantaneous Child

———————— ✥ ————————

Le poème est l'enfant instantané de la copulation entre le poète et les feux follets de l'inspiration.

The poem is the instantaneous child of the copulation between the poet and the fleeting flames of inspiration.

To Read Poetry

To read poetry
Is to drink
From eternity's spring
And every day
Is a good day
To sip the potent elixir.

Surrounded by Singing Birds

Lucky is the poet
Surrounded by singing birds.
He needs not struggle
To find a rhythm
To his poems.
They can simply take
The rhythm of the birds' songs.

Evening Mist

Evening mist dangling
Inside a luminous tunnel
Poetic essence spiraling
Inside creativity's well.

Wings Flapping Mosquito

Wings flapping mosquito
Gulping the poet's blood.
Are you trying to avenge
Your brothers and sisters
That the poet's books
Have flattened and killed?
Or are you an intelligent vampire
Trying to steal the poetic essence?

I lick the Spine

I lick the spine
Of each good poetry book
I read
And the muse's lips
Are the only lips
I kiss.

The Gods Pressured His erect Frame

The gods pressured his erect frame
Into the vertical mass of rock
They sealed arms legs and neck
Dark architects
Cut a sinister mirror
In which rows of white crosses
Stood inside circles
Of flickering flames
Like a suicidal butterfly
A heathen angel
In love with hell
Hovered and kissed each cross
And during each kiss
A deadly spear pierced
The winged creature's body
Blood shrouded red the crosses
The flickering hot tongues
 Licked the red crosses
Into whirls of hopeless images

The Monster-Tree

I did
I did see
The monster- tree
Of ultimate poetry
Its limbs were golden
And their ends spears
And they leaned
And bent down
And struggled
To write poems
Upside down poems
On the golden trunk
Which spewed blood-

I did
I did see
The vertical collection
Of upside down poems
Whose blinding words
Oozed out streamlets
Golden and bloody....

I knew the divine was in you

The very first day your graceful silhouette
Glided into the room
I understood that there was in you
An abundant river of poetry.
I saw in your movements
The grace of a cosmic goddess
Floating upon silent clouds.
I saw in your youthful eyes
Troubling images of rhythmic flows.
I heard in your scanning voice
The rumbling of primordial songs.
And I felt a burning desire to touch
The convoluted web of wonderful visions
That formed your blinding aura.
I saw in you a tumultuous river of poetry
Spewing from a pristine spring.

My Poems Are Lucky

My poems are lucky
A woman I love
And who does not love me
Loves them
Her hands hold them always
And hug them
And press them against her heart
She memorizes all their sweetest words
She falls asleep at night with them
And wakes up in morning with them
My poems are lucky
A lot luckier than I am.

Imploding Poems

I foresee
I foresee the time
When my poems implode
And become
Literary black holes
Disintegrating
The clinging fingers of gravity
In an all-expanding
Literary cosmos.

The Muse

She takes possession
Of you without your approbation
And you must follow with passion
The trend of her elucubrations

She awakes you at night
Whenever she desires
And you must be ready to eternize
Her weird desires

She loves to see rivers of tears
To give you hard times
For a thousand nights
Before she gives
A quick smile
And a drop of happiness

To be her host
Is to follow her
Wherever she goes
And promiscuous she flirts
Even with nothingness

She is a magic butterfly
Which unveils
With the simple touch of her wings
The universe's secret beauties

I Don't Write Poetry

I don't write poetry
My poems
Write themselves
Using my pen
And my right hand
And they are quite right
I don't write poetry
I could never write them myself

Woodlawn's Songbird and the Poet

Green little songbird
Sing your song
Atop the evergreen tree
Of greener Woodlawn
For the poet jogging
 With a green suit
On the green lawn
Of Indian Fields

Sing! Sing, green songbird!
And let the poet's verses
Rise and fall and jog
To the rhythm of your song!
Sing, green songbird! Sing!

The Pen of the Poet

The pen of the poet
Must be a catcher of comets
For the most beautiful thoughts
The most beautiful verses
The most beautiful visions
Arrive as comets
Streaking in the sky
And all, all of them
Must be written down
Even on scraps of paper

This rubbing cat

This cat rubbing herself
Against the poet's leg
Longs to say "Poem"
Instead of "Meow".

There is a vine called poetry

You and I were sitting
In front of a desk.
I recited my poetry to you,
You recited your poetry to me.
And then without knowing
What we were doing
We stood up together
To hug each other.
Without knowing how it happened
Our lips met.
In spite of all of our effort,
We could not separate them.

Since then, we understood
That there was really a vine,
A vine with big roots, big knots,
A vine with beautiful leaves,
Beautiful flowers and fruits,
A vine called poetry
Which unites our bodies
And souls,
Our lives
And destinies together.

After the Rain

That ballooned raindrop
Dangling from the apple
Waits for the poet's eyeballs
To catch its fall.

"If..." Seven Times

If your eyes cannot see
The wisdom spiral
In the stormy eye of the wind

If your eyes cannot catch
The friendly teardrop
Dangling from the eye of lightning

If your eyes cannot detect
The tall, telling smirk
On the colored lips of rainbows

If your eyes cannot perceive
The reflections of tender words
Bouncing inside a thunderbolt

If your eyes cannot read
The hidden message
At the inner core of each star

If your eyes cannot fish
The soothing love potion
From the churning depths of raging seas

If your eyes cannot immortalize
The fleeting games of sunrays
Upon the inside wall of your house

Then, you are not a real poet

La Clé Poétique

Comme du sable mouvant
Elle est fluide et mouvante.
Comme une tige d'or
Elle est dorée et éblouissante.
Comme toute chose enchantée
Elle est aveuglante et évanescente.
Elle fait le va-et-vient
Dans le vide divin
De l'ultime creation,
Et frôle, seulement
De temps en temps,
L'imagination
Des bardes vraiment
Marqués par le destin.
La clé poétique,
Aucune main
Ne la détient.
Aucune main!

A Poem Laments

This is the seventh time
I am being mailed
I am tired
Of being enclosed
Into envelopes
Tired of being dropped
Into mail boxes,
Tired of being unfolded
And put right away
Into SASES

This time again
I know I shall return.
It is awful
To be an unlucky poem.
I often compare myself
To an ugly child:
Only the mind which conceived me
Seems to love me

Words

Words
Words of flesh
Of flesh and blood
Of blood and fire
Of fire and life
Words uttered
With blazing capsules
What is the essence
Of the angry flames
Thundering
Inside the deep cauldrons
Of the primordial wombs?

Words

The Muse's Tongue

My tongue
Caresses
Only one tongue
The muse's
Tongue.

Poetry Honeycomb

Often nights
I wake up
To find poetry's honeycomb
Warm and rubbing itself
Against my lips
And my luscious tongue
Sucking and sucking
The sweetest essence.

My Muse Moans and Moans

When my muse
Moans and moans
Inside my eardrums
My pregnant poetic moon
Gently glides down
Sweetly opens her bosom
And bleeds and bleeds
And orgasmic poems
Explode and explode.

When my muse
Moans and moans

Disappearing Moons

Oh, these sweet little moons!
They tease my eyes
And my heart.
They tease my poetic essence.
They raise sweet little waves
In my poetic sea.
Oh, these vanishing little moons!

Primordialism

The last letter
Of the poem's first verse
DRIPS
The red fluid
Of primordial creation
Like blood dripping
From a wounded bird's beak.

Head down
Like a child
Inside a laboring womb
The poem creeps
        And CREEPS
In the poet's mind…

Isosceles Poem

He found himself
Changed
Into a poem
Divided
By its main verse
Into two similar
Isosceles
Triangles....!

Bi-Triangular Title

Inside the rich
Supergeometry
Of his brain
He saw
A poem
With two triangles
Of primordial symmetry
After the title
And no author's name..!

Semences d'Or in the Den

In the den of a denizen
Slicing shadows
into lascivious loaves
The dreams went wild.
Each neuron of the denizen's brain
Flashed on the den's walls
Uprooted oak trees
Hanging roots up and tops down
With thousands of hemorrhaging limbs-

The denizen stumbled
Into an eerie circle
With three different centers
Whose radii were warring shafts of light
Blocking blinding bending each other.
All tangent lines
Curled into agonizing rainbows!-

And like a ripe juice-filled grapefruit
Attacked by a devilish woodpecker
The denizen's heart bled and bled
Crisscrossed by the deadly swords
Of apocalyptic warriors-
Yet he cracked open his skull
And with both hands placed his throbbing brain
In front of his bulging eyeballs.

The membrane shielding the rich supergeometry
Pulsated pulsated with elemental rhythm
And like an exploding fruit
Erupted and disseminated protean gold nuggets
Precious seeds of the growing tree
OF UNIVERSAL LOVE..!

The Poem

The poem was on a table
A poem in black ink
On green paper
I was humming an old tune
A tune my old folks used to hum
The poem turned into a body
A wondrous body full of life
And the tune I was humming
Became a veil
A golden veil covering
The living poem
Two patriarchs arrived
Each one with a stethoscope
One auscultated my heart
The other the poem's heart
The poem's heart and my heart
Had the same rhythm

The Poet's Shadow

His shadow
Drifting behind him
As if floating
Upon a tormented sea
Forms a huge question mark
Which, from time to time,
Unwinds its curved top
And turns into
A big exclamation sign.

Literary Tug-of War

I turn and turn around the shadow
And the shadow turns and turns around me.

I tiptoe and tiptoe upon the shadow
And the shadow tiptoes and tiptoes upon me.

I blend and blend with the shadow
And the shadow blends and blends with me.

I become the shadow
And the shadow becomes me.

And the man-shadow
And the shadowy man
Become engaged in a literary tug-of-war
Inside the lettered links
Of a strange, funny fence.

Naked!

Naked!
He saw himself naked!
Totally naked!
In front of his typewriter,
Upon a shining, pitch-black high-chair
Mirroring weeping gods' heads-
His erected penis,
Spitting head of a rampaging cobra,
Swings up and down,
Left and right
Snapping keys printing
In bold black letters
Humankind's hidden essence.

Longing

The poet's eyes
Shed tears
Each time he feels
He would like
To become insane
To dive deeper
Into the poetic abyss
And he realizes
He cannot become insane

No Tall Tale!

I had just fallen asleep
When the poetry competition began
My uncontrolled brains
Ran up three poems
The first one on a boy
Being raped by his mom
The second one on a boy
Being raped by his dad
The third one on a boy
Being raped by himself

The third poem won the contest
And I woke up wondering
What the hell had happened.

Insane Man

Insane
That poor guy
Became insane
Insane
Of that rare type of insanity
Insane
Of an insanity
Which hunts
Stars
Comets
And peace
And love
And he goes around
Shouting
Always shouting
Shouting always
Three weird words
Three insane words
Never in the same order
Poetry poem poet
Poem poet poetry
Poet poetry poem

The poor guy
Became insane

His Pen..

His pen..
Rotating
In the center
Of a neon-lit V
Ejaculated
Gold…!

Poetic Gems

Poetic gems
Contains no germs.
They are crystallized poems.
Dew-drops
In morning sunlight.

Little Squirrel

Little squirrel,
You disturb my mind.
This tree
Is not a fruit-tree
And you climb it up
Climb it down
And climb it up
Climb it down.
Would you also climb
My poetry?
My muse dreams to feel
Your swift furry feet
To compare them
To the rhythmic feet
Of my poems.
Would you climb my poetry?

Her Song and My poem

She will sing me a song
And I will recite her a poem.
The words of my poem
Will waltz and tango
With the words of her song
The melody of her song
Will rise and fall
With the rhythm of my poem.
And my poem
And her song
Will be the loving symphony
In a lovely concert
Of two loving hearts.

She will sing me a song
And I will recite her a poem.

Lucky!!!

I have found my master key!
It had been hidden
Inside a book of poetry.
I am definitely lucky:
I may now unlock
All the glittering verses
Wiggling and wiggling
Like schools of colorful worms
Inside my skull's dark inner walls.
A key to unlock poetry!
I am lucky, definitely.

Le Cercle Des Anges (Club of Angels)

Ring ring seven seven seven
Ten eleven and then listen
Listen to an ancient poem
Written inside a forbidden den
With a pen stolen
From a newfound friend-

Listen! The drunken hands of an untamed denizen
Cruising cavernous dead-ends
Christened every single word-string-

Listen! Luscious female shadows
Glide upon ponds
Of heaven-scented clouds
And soar and hover and circle
The chosen words
Like guinea hens circling tree-tops
Where tired mates dream-

Listen! The germinal rhythm
Bends even hell's red flames
And quickens blood
In the devil's uneven vessels
And green and red and purple lights
During each lull reveal heavy hands
Cuddling ice cold beer cans and frozen

smiles of honeying workmen
With dead lobsters' eyeballs-

Ring and ring and ring and listen
Listen to the moving tale
Of an unsung denizen
In the dead of the night venturing
Into a No Man's Land..!

The Gift of Creativity

That "ombre de cactus'"
It appeared suddenly
On the pink wall.
Symmetric small hexagons
Composed its stem
And a perfect circle, its crown.
A real moon cactus
Grew in a fancy flower pot
On a metallic desk
Three feet away.
The priest lifted
The sacred sprout adoringly,
Like a Monstrance.
But, the shadow stood still.
The setting sun of autumn,
The gold vines of the willow,
The Venetian slats of the window
Had created a natural wonder
In the priestess' den

Where are the Gods?

Eleven times
The sound laden gong struck
The MASSIVE DEATH STAR
Raped the cosmic clock
Until the zero era.
Zero era
Time of disappearance
Of constructed titans
Dawn when decent humans
Stand and dance!

She reaches the titanic gods.
Her forceful fingers
Like ten red hot steel spikes
Penetrate the heavenly fleshes.
The flesh-scented smokes
Rise, ring, filter
And vanish
Into her hairy nostrils,
Reach the darkest caverns
Of her medusa skull,
Entrance millions
Of vicious vipers
Playing hide and seek
With the ultimate venom.

The cremation of the gods
Incenses rapturously
The heavenly architect
During her weird acts of CREATION!

Three Guitars

Three shadows
Of the adventurous bird
Glide on the span's pinnacle
Heaven designs
Nature labors
Crashing crystals
Kiss still steels
Shaking hands
With lightning
The deeps frogbird
Lights create
Absolute masters
Shadows hum
Exploding balls' songs
Difficult journey
She longs for a plateau
Where maids grow lilies
Haunted perspectives tangle
In her rear-eyeballs' rectangles
Her obsidian chest nurtures
Turbulent passion flower jungles
The sun dies red death
Her frontal antennas blend
Futures presents
Coagulate dawns' sunsets' golds
In noon's red cauldron

Her violet arrows
Bleed red
The moons' wombs
And the thrilled stars' heads
The boulders
Of the dead season's tombs
Roll and explode
Into the red REDNOON
Three guitars
Three silhouettes
Nine fingers
Songs and silences
Lights and shades
Lights and songs
Shades and silences
Heathen winds
Rape holy mountains
During menstruation's moon
Their gusts tunnels
Are always doubly red
And there is always a hum.

Necropsying

No bone
No flesh
Simply an estrous rhythm
In search of a heartbeat
To generate harmony.
 Streams of blood
Run on the concrete pavements
Drip from the edges
 Of the span
Slash in the deep darkness
Of old putrid waters.
The sky hides its blue moons
Heaven does not record
The crushing of life.
Tar and aloe
Keep clean the walls
Of the mysterious cavern
Echoing the steps
Of the mythical journey.
Life and love lurk
On the disease stricken walls
And the reflection of an Edenic mural
Decorating the den
Of a keeper of life
Can always bee seen
In the heliocentric pond.

But, there it is, a heathen hum
Undisturbed by the creaking of wreckages
A necromancy in a carbonous necropolis
Unstopped by the tock tock tock
Upon the dark drifting twin of the Styx

A Green Star for the Bard

In the mighty priestess' den
The denizen journeyed
To find his ultimate star
He saw twenty-one thunderbolts
Hewing twenty-one dead willows
With a raped man
Chained to each dead trunk
And weeping widow
Chained to each dead limb
He saw his own rooted out head
Planted upon
A wandering cactus'
Massive quartz-goad
Above these ancient shoots
A patch of sky
Like hell's mirror
Where all heathens
Contemplate
Their intimate selves
Hovered
With his skull's image magnified
Two thousand and two times
Horrified
He saw hell's belly
Landing
And gulping his skull

Quartz-goad
And moon cactus
And the priestess standing
Tall naked and red
Upon the nebula's dark side
With a huge green star
Whirling
At the tip of her luscious tongue......

Prelude

Seven "studstrikes"
Of the three primeval fires
Whipped his chest
Slashed his back
He melted sweetly
And melodies unheard before
Lulled even
The deepest eardrum-

The primeval heats
Melted him
Into blacksmith
And then wordsmith
And his luth struck
And its echoes
Entranced all molecules
On the Milky Way-

He journeyed beyond
The heavens' quicksand seas
Wandered into a crape valley
Kingdom of sidewinder reptiles
Atop the grim ridges of darkness
A priestess with a gold tooth
Hammered a heavy bronze gate
Upon his toes-

But thirteen moons ago
He was the chosen voyeur
Of the celestial orgy
Between the Divine Child
And the Holy Mother
The entire sky
Of a crucified land
Was their deep waterbed
And there were his own orgies
Orgies with the silex maiden
Since his seventh birthday-

The drive shaft
Whose nascent vibrations
Eroded sweetly deadly edges
Could salve and quench
The hottest bronze furnace
Endure the rottenest kiss
And suck the venom
Of the poison-laden tongue-

Golden Cross
Sacred relic
Of the ongoing godly Orgasms
Summon your eternal Nails
Your eternal Sledges
To hammer into the denizen's soul
The eternal DNA
Of the wanton Gods-

Journey One

Face turned to the right
Eyes looking South-West
Where does the speaker stand?
Ant one heading East
Ant two heading North
Plunges into the hole
Dug with a hoe
By an eleven-year-old mind
Waltz of the flies
Upon a spot
Vacant?
Little creatures
Are a lot more sophisticate
Than giant apes
Ant three heading South
Carrying a heavy load
Animalistic intuition
The winter of darkness
Failure of reincarnation
Of the burning fingers
Dead father time
And an empty saucer
On his right knee
Hands soiled
With egg-yolk
The sleeping child

Turns his cheeks
To the mounting breeze
The night crawler
Has not found yet
 A cool and damp cave
To coil its lewd length
The forgotten creature
The six-legged-rectangular-insect
Sheltering itself
Under the beach ball
Of the child
Talk of wood-peckers
At work
By five in the morning
Waking up
The old man
Who thought
It was
 His alarm clock
Talk of pregnant wild cats
Sneaking
Under garage doors
Talk of barbed wire
Talk of poison containers
To be bought
Old hands don't kill
A little ball
Leaves
 The forehead
Rolls

Just between his eyes
Follows
His nasal overpass
Falls
On his upper lip
Bounces
To his lower lip
Journeys
Down his chin
The fatal fall
Upon his hairy chest
So much creativeness
In the sun
It burns
Many mindful conceptions
Good bye
Old fan
Old hands
Cannot fix
And my busy fingers
Won't rebuild
Your burned out motor
And I tasted hell
And found it sweet.......

Journey Two

Touch...touch....touch
Touch softly
Little girls' thighs
Form little tunnels
Of very fragile crystals
Yellow pink
Red violet
Little crawling monsters
On white labels
Close tightly
A...numbers
B...numbers
C...numbers
Numbers A
By
Numbers B
By
Numbers C
Enough
To antiquate ASTROPHYSICS
The call of nature
Who worships her?
Not when corn and wheat
Grow at the bottom
Of the ocean
The asperities

Of bloody teeth
Across the ages' deepness
The denizens
Have become
The wild men of China
Their orgiastic dances
Are rhythmized no more
By the raucous music
Of bamboos
The deadly mechanical jaws
Chew
The TWENTY-FIRST embryos
The cup is empty
And the fumes
Of the steaming
Coffee and liquor
Dwindle agonizingly
Before the chunks of hearts
Coffee and liquor
Liquor and coffee
Chunks of hearts
Yellowish white
Inside
Light blue
Outside
Matching
The plastic cloth
Covering
An orange sky
Realization

Of diseased minds
Long…long
For the rebirth of Atlas
Silver circles
Crystal floors
Circle the floors
With silver and crystal
The adjoining snake
Spiraling vertically
The monstrous lips
Hold
Orange one
On the last story
Orange two
And apple one
On the second story
Orange three
And apple two
And capsule one
And cellule one
On the first story
The "rez-de-chaussée" is vacant
Insane "concierge"
Answer
Are you present?
Absent>
Alive?
Dead?
Weeping in solitude?
Drill a whole

Into the thinking skull
And hook up
Your electrode
On the chart
The love's line
Will not vacillate
From the coordinates zero
Love is dead
But buried regretfully
Like the hatchet
Of a warmonger
Where is the EVE
To accept the blessed FRUIT
From the divine lips
Of the passionate CHERUB
The FRUIT to be interred
With its kneeling seeds

The FRUIT to root split open
In one billion and one places
The hard crust of our cosmos
And grow to become
THE TREE OF SCIENCE AND GOOD…

The Radiant Line

A straight, radiant line
Lengthens itself
But stops
Just before touching
The lower limb
Of a golden C.

But, like a furtive smile,
The golden C
Fades away.

The radiant line
Retracts slowly
And curls itself
Into a glowing circle.

The Orgy of the Fools and the Suffering Maid

"il était là
Sur l'étagère
Le recueil de poésie
Tout couvert de poussière
Aucune main ne le touchait."

Tic…tac
Tic..tac
The passage of time
Indicating pulsing life?

Tic…tac
Tic…tac
Her heart shrieks
At each tic
At each tac.

The orgy of the fools
Does not stop
The luminescence of neon
Has defeated the sun.

Tic…tac
Tic…tac
The silhouettes move back and forth
They sway left

They sway right
They draw hundreds
Of blind curves
Over the flowered squares
Of the mirror of PROTEUS.

And tic…tac
And tic..tac
And there she lies
"La Douce Douloureuse
Pupilles closes"

Like all beauties
 Under an evil spell

Silhouette 1
Dares the first move
Places the thumb
Between her lips
But recalls the aphrodisiac
Of "la ronde des idiots."

Tic…tac
Silhouette 5
Gently leans
Places the little finger
Perpendicular
To the sorrowful virgin's lips…
The aphrodisiac
Of "la ronde des idiots!"

Tic…tac
Silhouette 3
And the middle finger
Machine made wand
Has no divine power
The aphrodisiac
Of "la ronde des idiots!"

Tic…tac
Tic..tac
Silhouette 2
And silhouette 4
The index finger
And the ring finger
Tic…tac
And tic…tac
The parted lips
Reclose soon
The aphrodisiac
Of "la ronde des idiots!"

"Le coma de la Douce Douloureuse continue"
And silhouette 5's hands
And silhouette 4's hand
And silhouette 1's hand-
Silhouette 2's hands
And silhouette 1's hand
And silhouette 3's hand
And silhouette 4's hand_
No opening for a vanishing species!
"Le coma de la Douce Douloureuse continue."

The Deaf Girl

Once, I saw a girl in a park.
I went to sit down near her,
Close enough to be heard,
And recited every single verse
I could remember…

When my memory ran dry…
When my lips stopped moving
And my voice fell silent
A hand touched my shoulder
And a voice said: "She is deaf"…

New Year 2005

In the first morning of the new year
Conscious that the world faces troubled times
I woke up with burning tears
Bursting from my eyes.
But soon a smile crawled on my lips.
A bold smile teasing the worst of times.
I had remembered suddenly
That I had my poetry
My divine weapon against infamy.

We Take Good Care of our Trees

We take good care of our trees
Whose limbs bend
Under the weight of their fruits;
And we neglect our poets
Whose hearts bleed
Under the heavy burden of poetry.

Each Month of May

—————— ✦ ——————

Each month of May
The muse and the Poet
Celebrate
Their fruitful journey-
Together they ride
A white little donkey
With two white baskets
Where two red bouquets
Grow wild…!

Twenty-Four Bull-Shaped Bells Atop the Span

As a lizard
Fearful of a dormant pool
At its tree's roots
Crawls back up
To find haven
Upon the top branches,
Head down he climbed
The stunning structure-
Silently, he screwed
Twenty-four bull-shaped bells
Creating a wondrous circle
At the misty tower's pinnacle

Then the soaring span swayed
And all the bells rang, rang, and rang-
Ringing the minute-hours of the span,
Ringing the day-nights of the span,
Ringing the zooming rays
Copulating thunderously
With the shrouding mist
And bouncing deep down
His skull's innermost recess
And into the fleeting wombs underneath-

Head down,
Like a stunned chameleon,

He glued his red eyeballs
To his BEING'S altered essence…!

And the stunning span swayed
And the bull-shaped bells rang!

Let the Daemon Have His Fire

A monster inside him!
Inside him there is a monster
A monster which drinks
Only a drink of fire
A fiery drink
They call poetry
His thirst is never quenched
No matter how much he drinks
He turns him into a seer
An insane seer
Who is always juggling
With letters words and sounds
With images dreams and visions
A seer rattling a magic jar
Of many colors
A foreseer with a niche
Of thunder-hatched verses
Laden with dreams from hell
Laden with god-spit curses
A seer-voyeur
Who makes verses poems poetry
Swing and sway
Like rainbow snakes
Dancing upon the master Vodou symbol (Vèvè)
A seer child of unsung ancestors
Who also had served the enraged daemon

Harnessing him and riding him
There is inside him a daemon
Who drinks flames of fire
His daemon requests fire
Give him fire

The Haitian Poet

Our poet is
A vodou priest
Who makes words
Sound like conch-shells
 Who makes words
Sound like bamboo trumpets
And who turns words
Into beautiful Rada drumbeat

Out poet is a wizard
Who juggles
Wondrous literary sounds
Inside a magic jar
A wizard who knows how to twirl
The most beautiful words
Who knows how to jam
The small drum of heavenly sounds
And who knows how to sing the blues
On the tip of his mother tongue
Until all priestesses, all angels
And all souls become possessed

Our men and women poets
Are shining masters of midnight
Who draw magic symbols
at the crossroads

Of knowledge
With the sacred dust
Of all gone master poets

I Snatched the Zombie of a Beautiful Poem

———— ✦ ————

I am buried
Standing up
In a cemetery
For people with creative minds.

The zombie
Of a beautiful poem
Which lost its place
Wanders in the cemetery
Like an ill-fated butterfly.

It goes from
Skull to skull
Until it enters inside
My own skull.

I welcome the zombie
Of the poem
And place it inside
My heart's most sacred vessel.

It is why
My soul is always strolling
In the most beautiful garden
Of poetry.

Do not fly away, Doves

Doves, do not fly away.
The foot-steps you hear
Are the foot-steps of a poet
Do not fly away, doves
His chest holds
As much love
As your chest.

The Denizen Begged

The denizen begged a pretty girl
With wondrous lips
To recite him a poem.
The wondrous lips smiled
And whispered:
" I don't know any poem.
I have never met a poet."

A Robin Red-breast

A robin red-breast
Quenching its thirst
From the denizen's pail!
After, will it sing the denizen's songs
Or, will the denizen imitate its songs?

On the Denizen's Path

On the denizen's path
A kneeling pen!
Poems praying
To be written.

As Simple as a Nipple

I am a poem as simple
As a nipple
And like a nipple
I create divine ripples

Poetry, the never tamed horse of a true poet.

Short Poems/Long Poems

Short poems
I love them
They easily enter my mind
And quickly become mine
I love short poems.

Long poems are mighty rivers
Whose raging flows
Transport us to amazing corners
Of the poet's brain

I Am a Poem

I am a poem
Unwritten
Write me
I will be your poem.

I am a song
Unsung
Sing me
I will be your song

I am looking for a dream and a song

I am looking
I am looking
For a dream
A dream and a song
A dream I lost
And a song I heard
In that dream

I am looking
For a dream
And a song

It is always high noon

It is always high noon
In a real poet's room
The true poetic mind
Does not recognize midnight

Some of the poems in this book had appeared in " A KISS TO THE LAND" published by SubPress in 2017 with Antonino D'Ambrosio and Greg Fuchs as Editors.

About the Author

Son of humble peasants, Denize Lauture left Haiti in 1968. He was then a machinist and welder, and had not graduated from high school. He worked as a welder in Harlem and attended evening classes at The City College of New York

He received a B.A. in Sociology in 1977, a M.S. in Bilingual Education at CCNY; and a M.A. in Spanish Literature at Lehman College. Additional graduate studies at Fordham University and at the Graduate Center of CUNY.

He writes in Haitian Creole, English and French. He has published more than a dozen books. Children's books with Penguin Putnam, Simon and Schuster and Educavision; poetry in English with SubPress,New York: A Kiss to the Land, 2017, The Black Warrior and Other Poems, 2005; two major French books: Les dards empoisonnes du denizen (2015), Les Lunes d'or du cactus (2017) with the Trilingual Press in Boston. He also published four books in his native language and Denizens of Hope, a bilingual book, with CC Marimbo (2015) Berkeley, CA. His latest book is LAURORE, a Boy Bright and Bold, which is a novel in verse by Amazon.com, 2024.

In collaboration with Stephen Motika, Director of Readings, he helped organize a day of Haitian Poetry and music at Poets House in New York in 2010. Four well known Haitian poets were invited.

He never stops being involved in the struggle for progress in his native land. During his literary visits to Vassar College, N.Y., he met Dr. Andrew Meade who helped him contact Pure Water for the World. Pure Water for the World introduced Denize's handpicked contacts in Haiti to Water for Life which in turn negotiated with Foods for the Poor; and now, there are sixteen artesian wells in the region where he was born. Also, he recently sent 45 boxes of books to a small library he helped create in a school located in his birthplace region. He is the founder of Total Kindness LLC.

Some of his poems have appeared in:

Artist and Influence, (Hatch-Billops Collection)

Black American Literature Forum (Indiana State University)

Callaloo, Johns Hopkins University

Liberation Poetry (Trilingual Press)

Illuminations (College of Charleston)

The Poetry of Everyday Life, (City Lore, New York)

Capitals, an anthology about the cities Capitals of the world

Musings about the pandemic, a global anthology published in Kenya.

He is one of the three editors of THIS LAND, MY BELOVED, a trilingual anthology of Haitian poetry, 2023, Trilingual Press, Boston.

Denize lives in the Bronx, New York and taught Haitian Creole and Culture, Bilingual Education, French Language and Literature, Spanish Language at Saint Thomas Aquinas College, New York.

The book with Penguin Putnam is FATHER AND SON (1991). It was nominated to the NAACP'S Images Awards.

The book with Simon and Schuster is RUNNING THE ROAD TO ABC (1996). It won the Coretta Scott King Award.

Denize most recent book is "THE ONEIRIC JOURNEYS OF THE DENIZEN AND SOME THOUGHTS ON KINDNESS" published by Hawes and Jenkins in June.